Frédéric Delalot

washingtonias and zoetropes 2

KDP Editions

Precious eras...

I remember, I was going out...

I went through the weeks

Happy fantasy, hope

Long sequence, images

I had been a traveler...

Coves, full heat, and landscapes...

Old novels, limit of sleep...

Returning to Montreal, imbued with an emotion.

The penumbra was pierced by the stars

Happiness, fortuitous ride...

I sometimes came back, with a look...

I was driving in the massif...

It was the perfect time...

At the edge of the world, and on the moons

Mosaic of temptations, allies...

Caresses like turns...

While years had passed, nonchalance

Describe the progress, just a moment...

Decorated with old-fashioned tags...

Presumably heat shifted...

Birds flew away

Months and years...

Bohemian blend...

How long will it take...

And I was thinking about our roads, and the endless terraces.

There was music...

In the present of the Earth...

Like desires...

The party was moving...

Idyllic attractions...

In parks or lounges

That's it, the years passed

In appearance, forms of time

Like unfinished loves

Decades...

I didn't want to rush anything...

I had woken up in this world

Interconnected, the next day...

I had gone in the general direction...

Studies, construction...

Tomorrow is the solstice

Summer, in Montreal...

Precious eras...

With other archives...

Decades passed.

Years of total love

Founding elements...

Of the future, lights...

Reds, from the Square...

Stones and wefts, planet...

I remember, I was going out...

From a building, on the horizon...

The giants of the future anchored themselves

Of a much superior intelligence

To ours, space, flower pots...

Minishort in pink sequins...

Eternity, garden, anchor point...

From this reality...

Towards happiness, on deck...

Marie, connecting Île Saint-Louis

At the Quai de l'Hôtel-de-Ville...

Trails, sums of reflections...

I went through the weeks

Look for old photos

From my youth, maple sugar...

And by this approach...

News, sand clouds

Curtain of heaven, at night...

I was rebuilding the décor

From this period

Rather fir trees...

Red lights

In the park...

3

Freedom, dislodged from the dark skies...

Integrated compromises, smelled like paper

Luxury, notebooks, reflection of years, already...

As long as our bodies get drunk...

Mind-blowing ships, embarking

The invincible force of summers...

Happy fantasy, hope...

Projects, boil in the thirties

Flower headband, weekend.

Emblematic church

Peacemaker Christmas...

And New Year's Day, salon

New geometries

Watercolors, courses

On screens...

There was Midnight Romeo...

Winter coats, minus thirty

By the way, didn't I have

Sucked into relaxing...

Long sequence, images

From villages, on occasion...

Data entry...

In the distance, magnolias...

It was a very long time ago

To see the boats...

And the naves, in the evening...

I had been a traveler...

And party player, basically...

We were locals

You had to believe in the scrub...

I remembered her room...

In Nogent, leaves of the trees

Which flew away, deserted park

Replay on earth...

I read, recognition

Shapes, moments...

Of rapprochements...

I was reading...

We had hit the road

From a deep evening...

With friends, friends...

Glorious, magical flowerbeds

Sands with millenary plants

Coves, full heat, and landscapes...

The energy came back, recharged the curves...

I remembered a hotel on Saint-Paul Street.

Friends...

Faces in the unreal lair

Where the landscapes change...

Island, gregarious vehicles...

Some shiny night, when I read...

Old novels, limit of sleep...

Outside, the icy wind, maybe go out

We hummed When Doves Cry...

That year, old sweaters...

At the appointed time, far from the city center

Near the porch of a manor house...

We were talking about spherical villas...

Industrial design, muted

At Café Buade, on a Sunday...

We were rising to the edges...

There are so many pure instincts...

So, we were entitled to a share of carelessness...

Snowy spaces and roads, going to Quebec City...

Returning to Montreal, imbued with an emotion...

During the PyeongChang Winter Olympics

Extract of brushes, we drove at night ...

It was not necessary to delay, summaries more true ...

There had been elixirs in Barcelona, a gargote

It was a clear black night, a clear white moon...

What could they imagine

With regard to the alcoves...

Summers, springs...

The month of May...

Diaphanous blondes and torsos...

Muscular, the zero moment, the symbols...

At the scale of quantum experiments

Wanderings of a precious club, ocean...

A bit of Asia, it was always dark...

The penumbra was pierced by the stars

Rediscovering luck, awakened this time

In the heat, work of musicians...

After some Spanish hostel...

Hovering, throwing dreams, in the nettles

Sometimes, every line, every day...

Images of a mirror, memories...

Happiness, sometimes straddled by chance...

Games, timeless spring...

Strength of ramparts, very far away

Describe the steep descent

Which led to the activities...

Could we have cross-dressed...

The brilliance of the waves...

This set of blown adaptations

By ear, guardian of the world...

And I slept naked, on the rocks...
I sometimes came back, with a look
Contemplative, at sunset of the star
On the verge of exciting deraisons...

I remembered our youth
Prehistoric television, freedom...
Informal, mutual dense era...
Well after the ambient railings

Contrasts, movement
Within this time...
Bands, pairs...
Enrichment...

Last word...
Contours...
Between currents
Sheltered numbers...

I progressed by keys...

Harmless, regular...

Behind a peaceful curtain

Combination...

Liquor deckchair

Timeless...

I was driving in the massif

De la Clape, full moon

Sailing school in the sun.

Flying Dire Straits to Munich, Jean-Louis Murat...

Fly The Police or The Smiths, in the fields

In front of a car, she had the easy elegance...

Not to dwell on the extension of the stories...

Her hair was floating...

In the light wind...

It was the perfect time...

The time of simultaneity

She was out until dawn, she was sleeping

We found ourselves in Place Blanche, we danced...

In the distance, Old Montreal, suddenly...

After the rain, they walked on the leaves.

Sensual balance, calm

Serenity, the years...

Slowly, flowed...

I remembered her smile

Gradual metamorphosis

Memories, he had written

A date, next to a text

It's winter, I was reading...

The dream terraces, best summer...

Were emerging, banks, appointments...

At the edge of the world, and on the moons...

From Jupiter, we dreamed of snowy evenings

The warm corridors of the spaces...

Comforted the wait for a dawn

We were always levitating...

Above multiple crossings.

On the Square, in the corridors

There was the crowd of the Night...

It was a strange time...

A large circle included us...

Described a figure in space

And time, sculpted the Square...

There were twenty-five spheres...

Mosaic of temptations, allies...

I occasionally had images.

The Grande Sarabande on the way back

Caresses like turns

Enlightened, referred to our eyes...

The doors of memories, I read...

On the Square, ephemeral light

A logic illuminates these bays...

The youth went hunting...

Music of legendary cities

We were going, in the perfect heat

Discover the subtle progressions...

The lanterns dazzled us...

Standing, desert by the sea...

Xerophiles, we trampled triangles

Grass, at rest, under the panels...

I put on a burgundy sweatshirt, to go out

The City had removed the Ferris wheel...

Facades of architectural projection...

If they lit up in the galaxy to come...

New civilizations, perfect harmony

That's it, I thought I'd see other years again...

And there was a bit of Lovedrive...

A Time Machine...

For everything, a colossal wheel

Basically, we were locals

I had found old Rahan albums...

I was coming back to the height of St. James Square...

While years had passed, nonchalance

Then we slammed the doors, casual.

Dressed in colorful towels...

We see this liberated world...

Modulations, after history

Multitude of rare species...

On the way, I listen to the newsletter

Nothing trivial, whisper

Describe the progress, just a moment

Just a moment, the magnitude clears

The fullness of their protected future.

From a halo...

Quintessence...

Later landscape...

Where is the frame added

Trees, courtyards...

Robert Miles at Station C...

Shorts in black linen, sign...

Decorated with old-fashioned tags

Like images...

Nomadic coincidences...

A thousand pages, intermittency

Illusion, indefinite din ...

In the fog of an era...

Carnal vehicle, absolute values...

We retam theses, among others

And imagination unmasks reality...

The moving delirium of appearances...

Presumably heat shifted...

Exhume of words, axes, delicate bank

Hotel bar closed, at the edge of the diving board...

This mystical alliance can succeed

And sail life, primitive mystery ...

Original, our daily lives, beings...

The potential for a renaissance...

Things...

Relationships...

Overflowing...

Metamorphosis.

Heterogeneous canvases

Prime emotion...

The riders...

I was walking, the landscapes

The dispersals, offshore...

Brought me the form of the story

Outdoor world...

And birds flew away...

In the white sky, between the trees.

Daily

Far...

Real...

Slow motion...

Horizons, this coincidence...

Would mean a trip...

Months and years...

Rechargeable in an instant

Sand Loves

Magnetizations...

Unlikely...

Horizons...

Parallel paths...

Walks, in time...

Often, I had wanted a story

Faster or slower...

Light again...

Between the trees...

Getting drunk on a future

Radiant, discoveries

First time...

Bohemian blend

Colors...

And patterns...

Lolailolailolailolai / lolailolailolau...

Redo the tour, recreate the pleasures, the hopes

Letters I've written, never meaning to send...

When the world was asleep...

Elusive moments...

The balls bounced

The Stadium, the blue courts

Silky lanterns...

Reasons for attractions...

How long will it take

Everything would be travel

Circus troupe...

Black mini-skirts...

And on the old buffet under the gray dust

There is still a postcard...

Ah! many people came and went...

And we read the memory of fluids...

Tall trees, paths, wastelands

We could almost see them making the transition...

Those months had something essential...

And I was thinking about our roads, and the endless terraces.

Stories in space-time

According to a simple chronology

There were in the memory...

Retrospective waves...

Satiations, unsatisfied

All this in a big circle...

Secret coasts, cybernetic oasis...

And sand offered, almost projects

For a moment

The eternal expansion

Ring colors

In a kitsch way...

There was music

All day long...

Printed on the front...

For all, in white...

And, in other times...

There would be other lists

Did we know it then...

Another life...

There were dials, clocks

Digital, screens, the wheel...

Inspired by a mechanical box...

Hope fulfilled...

And our delights...

Technology and music

Clarity, as...

Let the future take root...

In the present of the Earth.

We would dance...

Close to the shores...

Narrow road...

Tournicoti tournicoton

Cap des voiliers...

We forgot ourselves

In the moment...

Like desires...

Momentary, lost...

Everyday atmosphere

Decade far away...

Years passed...

That was a long time ago

We were fir trees...

And service-stolen...

Meters from the shore...

Morning, espresso...

Many universes...

And through this setting

The party was moving

In our footsteps...

And she was waiting for me...

On the Tokyu Honten-dori

We were walking around...

Millennia...

Of rapprochements...

Still the exaltation...

Sensitive taverns.

We were looking to be similar...

To the memories of nonchalant happiness...

Irrepressible attractions, idyllic drunkenness

Sounding volutes...

Merovingian outfit...

Decades followed one another

And nights...

I remembered...

After seasons.

In parks or lounges...

With the landscapes, the paradises...

Ether, winning mistrals...

In the afternoon, we passed Grease

Or Kennedy Airport

Flying papers...

Michel Berger...

Daniel Balavoine...

Around...

From a cross

I stared at the sky...

And its ships...

The plots, the realities

Drowsiness...

To the west, to the north...

Recurring space...

That's it, the years passed

Like comings and goings...

I remembered the drunkenness...

The terraces, and it was good

We would like each other elsewhere...

Relationship that unfolded

From our dreams...

From the day before, really...

Landscapes...

Changes...

Underground corridor

To the Square...

13

The world would strive to shape

In appearance, forms of time...

Debonair perspective of writing...

Almost automatic reconciliations

Magnetizations, insatiable happiness...

Between improvisations and festivities...

Imagined it, then

Even for a short while...

Servers-volleyball players...

Years of carefree...

And beginnings...

How many millennia

Were we enjoyment...

Perfect harmony, that's the time...

We were looking to be similar...

Memories of nonchalant happiness

Like loves in suspense...

Roads that crossed the fields...

Where we had managed to imagine a sequel

Sunny, lives and things...

Curvatures, gravitation, infinite passages...

Stability

Soothing

Lights

Blue

As time goes on

Enveloped us...

Far, far from games

Abracadabrantesque...

Movement...

Decades

Montreal...

Underground...

Night...

Osmosis...

Alcohols...

Caravans...

14

In their sleep...

Again this voice...

What was that light?

We would dance...

Dressed, undressed

Like a party

I didn't want to rush anything

We could almost see them...

Making the transition...

Eternal form of the universe

Pictured life from yesterday

In the countryside, through it

I was looking at the past....

We would like to...

We would like to...

And then we listened

Electro-funk...

We slammed the doors

Faced with the impossible choice...

From a unique destiny...

All of a sudden, destination.

Bicoques of an exhibitionist district...

Transformed into swerves, worldliness...

Bronze molosses, caulked entrance...

She inquired about the motivations of the bivouac

Kept nothing on her...

Orange city, bare legs...

Tour of the calendars, I alternate...

I don't ask myself any more questions

Before the end of the party

Often, disobedient

Mirrors in the night...

Bright swimming pool...

I guessed the parallel life we would have lived

We wanted to keep falling in love with each other...

She had a turquoise tunic, very short...

Almost wise, we crossed paths a lot...

15

In the park, scents of promises

Outings and appointments...

From what we thought were random...

Dried leaves rolled behind me

And the party was fading, all this was far away...

And it was time to leave, perhaps...

With me, towards Place de la Bastille...

Chance brushing, dredging courses

In Phillips Square, new thoughts...

I must have been twenty years old

Desire to merge...

Outside ideas...

Extrapolate...

Ancient dream...

Plots of eternity...

Unity, Architecture

The palm of the hand...

In the story...

She was talking to me...

From a temple...

Which was watering us...

Ephemeral mix

To deliver...

Walks away...

In a hurry, June evening

Gigantic beaches

Detours of the mind...

At the helm of a chance

The road was bare...

And glorious frenzy...

Extravagance of happiness...

The city appeared, at the beginning

Trace of the evenings of the previous day

Inked pattern...

I had the taste...

Secret corners

Close to caravans.

16

Feast time

I swallow the wind...

Claims...

On the same day...

From the same month...

From the same year

Greenery surrounded the metropolis

Yesterday residents, dreamers by the way

And I fell asleep late...

Set with caches...

The architecture of things

The words of a laughing voice

At the edge of the expanses...

This azure as the bottom of things...

The comings and goings, countryside, metropolises

Memories, harmony of sleep...

I just had to let go of the hours...

We escaped from ourselves...

For other holidays...

The world was full of doors

Intoxicating, mantle of reality...

Other eras, in order to enjoy...

Nonchalances, masts of the Place

Unimportant, indefinite din

Illuminated the city at night

Beautiful black coffee...

The Opera was just a project...

The Square did not yet exist

Ah! as everything has changed...

The plaster paths

White, stepladders...

Imagining a world...

Watching, with friends

Raspberry trees...

Other gardens...

Calm snow...

Years later.

17

Dressed, undressed...

Similar partners...

Easy lightness, paroxysm

Memories became clear

Further, in space...

In the direction of Mars...

We weren't there yet...

Around me, photographs

My consciousness expresses the world.

By creating truths

Brought back from a space

I'm taking a train...

Landscapes parade

We play the same ephemeral game

I remember the first night

The music probably plays...

But it's just a dream...

There, for a brief moment...

A thousand years ago...

Relatively blurry landscape...

Ark of the world, at the borders.

From alley to alley...

Beyond the old blocks...

I caressed your abandonments...

Nocturnes, after terraces

Long hair that floats...

We needed the effects

In the center of the unknown islets...

In the middle of the posters...

Show of minutes...

Surfers, in this world...

Clouds, landscapes of wanderings...

Love sequences, seasons

Cavale against a backdrop of ecstasy...

Bearings, walkways...

Engraved, from a Peloponnese

Carefree, and naked, terraces...

18

Overlooking the sea...

At sunset, omen

Other whispers...

Exaltation

Short story...

Nocturnal...

Happiness at the top...

From a tower, Apache...

America of the cliffs...

Glass, extremes...

Latitude, worry-free evening...

Mischievous, benevolent lighthouse...

I draw potential, rebirth

Era of grandiose cities

Mountains, on the margins...

Time, strength of the rails

I was coming home from days...

Fearless...

Space naves...

Debauchery of energy...

Mist, world of asphalt.

Station platforms, which have become deserted

Virgin, creative lands...

Bankers crisscrossed...

The surroundings, at the time...

Cloud of exaltation...

Great fortune...

Attraction of avenues...

Now free space

Lesser adventures

Silver shores...

Perfect world...

And mystery...

Again, unreal happiness...

Interior light, curious

Behind the ramparts...

I stroked her skin...

19

Above multiple crossings

There was the crowd of the Night...

The lanterns dazzled us...

That's it, I thought I'd see more years again

A little trivial, whisper...

Like images...

The moving delirium of appearances

In the white sky, between the trees

Rechargeable in an instant...

Lolailolailolailolai / lolailolailolau...

Elusive moments...

Those months had something essential

Did we know it then...

There were dials, clocks

We forgot ourselves...

Meters from the shore...

Sounding volutes...

With the landscapes, the paradises...

The terraces, and it was good...

Magnetizations, insatiable happiness...

Curvatures, gravitation, infinite passages.

Lights...

Like a party...

All of a sudden, destination...

She had a turquoise tunic

And the party was fading, all this was far away

Desire to merge...

The road was bare...

And I fell asleep late...

Set with caches...

From other times, in order to enjoy

Easy lightness, paroxysm...

There, for a brief moment...

In the middle of the posters...

America of the cliffs...

Latitude, worry-free evening

Silver shores...